Outside Girl

by Cyndi Dawson

POETS WEAR PRADA • HOBOKEN, NJ

Outside Girl

First North American Publication 2010.

Many thanks to the magazines and anthologies that have published some of these poems: *A View from Here, Breadcrumb Scabs, Deep Tissue Magazine, Gloom Cupboard, Gutter Eloquence Magazine, Heroin Love Songs, Lines Written with a Razor, Off Beat Pulp, The Plebian Rag, Pushing The Envelope, Sparkbright, Spine Writer, Whisper & Scream Magazine,* and *63 Channels.*

ISBN 978-0-9841844-7-7

Printed in the U.S.A.

Front Cover Illustration: Rene i.a.t.b.a., who really IS the best artist, and was one of the fortifying forces of artful SoHo, NYC in its heyday. He now lives and creates in Brooklyn, NY. Vist him at www.reneiamthebestartist.com

Back Cover Author Photo: The Dawson Archives

Most of all,
I would like to thank Paul and Chelsea Dawson
for their love and generosity
throughout the process of writing this book.

Introduction

At seventeen I fled suburban New Jersey to live with a bunch of punk-rocker friends at a loft on the Lower East Side, and study acting at The Lee Strasberg Institute. A mutual friend introduced me to Rene, a Venezuelan artist who made string body sculptures called *Nudismos*.

Rene and I became each other's muses. He wove *Nudismos* onto my body and I read my poems aloud while we waited for the painted string to stiffen into sculpture. This evolved into a well-received performance piece, and the SoHo art world opened for me.

Between acting jobs I tended bar at a rock club, where I also performed on poetry night. One of the many musicians I met at the club, Jair-Rohm Parker Wells, became a close friend. It was only years later, while back in NJ, that these events became significant.

In 2007, out of the blue, Jair-Rohm emailed me from Stockholm to ask if I was still writing. Yes, I was.

We started collaborating online, Jair-Rohm creating music for poems I recorded for him, and next thing I knew we were doing live shows from London to NYC. I started a poetry series called Poets and Angels which introduced me to poets and musicians that initiated new creative collaborations. Poetry was always what drove me.

The poems in this book focus mainly on the 1980s—the "what came before." What comes after? I'm living it now. Stay tuned.

Cyndi Dawson

Contents

Introduction

Outside Girl by Rene

Color Wheels 1

Go Go 3

Defining Moment 4

A No-Heat Space 6

Black Leather Pants 7

A Beautiful Thing 8

Step Outside the Car 10

Love and Ecstasy 12

Jett in the Black Leather Coat 14

Exit 14 15

Resolution 17

How to View a Decade 18

A Slow Wet Thaw 19

The Passing of Things 21

Your God Forbids 22

Toddy Idol 23

Transition 24

Mustard Love Song 25

Doing the Math 26

Draw Me a Cover 27

About the Author

Color Wheels

Look, we were young.
Our eyes sang each other in,
ideas wild in
rivers of string
and paint.
You saw the stars in my eyes
as spotlights
on silver runways
and sirens washed along Jones Beach.
You draped me in aqua
and seafoam green
string seaweed,
sculpting my dreams
of mythical creatures
watery, mercurial...
Look, how your beard was black
as a crow,
your hair twisted into devil horns.
Around your neck hung
a cross cradling a vagina
which you said was less violent
than a man hung with nails
which you swore you did worship.
If you were meant to be
a tortured man
better it be
vaginas
than the face of a dying man.
Look, we were big kids
playing in playgrounds of canvas
and dialogue
spurring the other on.

Now your black beard is grey
but holds the texture of
decades
and it does not hide
or apologize for itself, nor
your eyes full of devilment
and rebellion.
Look,
that was us but us still
breathes color wheels
into sirens.
In your eyes
I am still on Jones Beach.
In your eyes
I am still
some mythical creature
watching you sketch our dreams
from points of lead
and scrap paper.

Go Go

This particular shift, smoked to fog.
Cigarettes, legal as crotches,
were aimed at chins and pockets.
Heat throbbed harder with every drink
poured from both nimble hands.

Precision.

Stilettos clicked stage floor,
girl in dressing room, needle stuck in arm,
livid at some cruelty of light.
Tequila, check. French fries. Check.
Vomit.
Call barback, mops and pine sol.

Precision.

Shake my ass, grab my tips.
Get dancer off floor littered with sequins.
Wipe blood off her g-string. Smack her awake.
Prop her back onto stage with puppet smile.
Grab my tips.

Precision.

Defining Moment

I fled my father's house
with a rock & roll boyfriend
who bathed in beer.
I married him
because nobody told me not to.

Walked into brand new club
with squared, cracked sign:

Patrix: Good Food, Live Music

My spandex ego
grasped at leather-clad boys,
inhaling freedom.

Behind that bar
I separated myself
into girl that was
and girl that was becoming,
poured cash prizes
alchemized into gold.
On the other side —
red light sweat of dance
and guitars.

New Brunswick swelled, clubs
flourished. Poets
gathered at the Roxy Grill
to spit out words
and knock back shots.
I had something to say

When left goes right.
When right feels so right
That direction is less a lesson
than an infusion of oxygen.

Friday: Matt Pinfield spinning
or some Jigs and The Pigs.
Saturday: Ivan Kral said I was cute.
Sunday: I wrote a poem for him
and read it at the Roxy.

A little girl's poem.

A No-Heat Space

We might have been listening to The Ramones
but God knows I have long term memory loss.
I knew you were high as Orpheus.
We skated through hallways,
imaginary blades connected with feet—
unaware of frigid air, this no-heat space.
Dishes stacked for days blended into stains
in an old porcelain sink.

It might have been you who said it first,
that only blocks away Sid had murdered Nancy.
You can't make this shit up. Something about it
seemed so romantic. Because you had
rockstar shoulders, necklaced by low slung guitar.
Because we were chemically parallel,
we were sailors coasting same city floors, tilted.
If you killed me now I might be famous, too.

Somebody turned on an amp. Then I heard it:
Her singing, from another room, siren in its
ennui, and I knew she would come rabid for you.
I knew if I slipped prostrate, glimpsed you,
beautiful with light slipping from pore and lip
that the way her hips changed with seconds
You would reverse coma a kiss for her
Hoping to tear skin, hoping it would end in blood.

Black Leather Pants

Do girls shed snakeskin for pretty boys with guitar faces?
I shed my flesh with speed and pills.

Everyone loves the girl slapping beer and shots.
Everyone loves the girl dancing to the beat

who can't say no
slipping tinfoil tips into tight black leather pants.

Yes, girls shed skin, conjure smiles for men
clenching powdered dollars with semen fingers.

They bend windows of cleavage, hit stainless steel
for quick white snorts hidden behind salt shakers.

Girls like me. Clever.
Clever as a hit off that spot between thumb and wrist.

Pretend to down shot of tequila
but the lick is a snort is a snort is a snort

is four days awake and two just for sleep,
crying in pillows of dry, peeling skin.

Do girls shed themselves for the strum of a song?
Yes. They do.

A Beautiful Thing

One night I went looking for love
in the bathroom of CBGB's.
My friend was in the stall next to me.
We pulled airplane liquor bottles
from our winter coat pockets
cause you never got to the bar
or the bartenders were just too busy.

Either way it made sense
to hide those little babies in our coats,
slug them in the stalls
where graffiti boasted who was available
or which bands sucked.

She pulled out the first bottle,
passed it under the stall over to me.
It was tequila — liquid rage.
The only time I beat someone bloody
was after five shots of tequila.

I pushed it back over,
grabbed the vodka from my own pocket.
It fell from my hand.
The liquor slow-mo'd out the top,
mixing with various human waste on the floor.
A girl screamed at me to hurry the fuck up.

I went looking for love but found no safe haven in the stall,
just a dirty cell deprived of my right to solitude
and a good buzz. I opened the door,
saw that chick leave her cocktail on the sink.

I let her into the stall.
Grabbed her glass. And back to the club.

Music radiated;
seeped into skin, my being, my every pore.
I knocked back the drink,
threw the glass into the corner with the others.

Love is a beautiful thing.

Step Outside the Car

Lynn had five hundred Quaaludes in a baggie.
Five of us had been swallowing them
for seven days.
Now the twenty or so left
sat on the driver's side of his disheveled Datsun
like mischievous children
taunting passersby to notice tough love style.

With sea legs we managed basics.
Food, to a minimum.
Short trips escaping safety of house
where I holed up with a boyfriend
I mostly disregarded. But he knew Lynn
more than me
which qualified my place
and guaranteed ongoing buzz.

We drove aimlessly, then spotted signs.
Sidewalk sales. Tables of items
calling to the rebels we'd discovered we were.
Shampoo. Toothpaste. Brushes.
Lynn pulled his car close to a curb,
rolled down his windows. Five sets of arms
reached out windows taking a tube, a bottle, a box.
No cash exchanged.

He drove away. Casually sweating.
Red lights flashed familiar behind us.
"Get out of the car. Slowly," voice said.
Unwanted boyfriend grabbed baggie
shoved it down unwashed pants.

I saw events unveil themselves in riddles
but I was untouchable.
"Left brake light is out," voice said.

Lynn was shaking, but not me.
Something was around me, shielding.
A layer of armor. Impenetrable.
I stayed cool where others crumbled.
This gift for numbness, courtesy of
a calculated survival instinct
grown from gypsy blood
and Lynn's bag of five hundred ludes.

Love and Ecstasy

You left me on the third floor of Danceteria,
Music television above my head
on multiple screens.
Ecstasy pulled me abruptly up, then down.
There, by the screeching elevator,
where trendy punks were spit out
in intervals, you said I betrayed you.

You, beautifully jealous after crossing
'The Velvet Rope'
your cheekbones our admission.
I was your girl,
you were my guy
us the 'WE'
as night raved on.

Left me there on that sleazy third floor
with the paper cup girls,
counting their change after busking on
St. Marks Place, their silly
skull-and-crossbones tattoos.

I stumbled down cracked exit stairs
to streets of a city
that always loved you more.

After you left me on the third floor of Danceteria.
You said I looked at someone else.
In a crowd of hundreds, with blood
pumping music in waves
both pulsing then slowing,
you made me feel the whore,
left me fending for myself.

And I completely loved you —
even back to Elmhurst
on that damned E train

Jett in the Black Leather Coat

Jett went bang bang bang,
whirled faster than everyone else.
Dealt the best coke at Danceteria
and after hours across the street:
a black-tiled private club where
customers shot up right at the bar.
Boys in ripped tee's, sleeves rolled like James Dean,
bony arms, pale skin, blond punk girlfriends.
Bathroom reeking of cat piss and old litter.
Gay boys mixing it up with straight boys.
Ambivalent girls with DJ's and doormen.

Jett was his own universe,
mixed with smack, mixed with coke,
mixed with ecstasy and any unattended drink.
Jett busked in Washington Square, played
a decrepit guitar so badly people paid him just to stop.
He'd take his tenner to cop, by nine he'd
bang bang bang his way across the loft, drink up all
our wine and start all over again.

There was never any toilet paper.
I wrote poems for the roaches to read over my shoulder.
Jett needled tracks across his arms, hid them
behind black leather sleeves. For a little while,
I thought I could save him.

Exit 14

In Jersey we Bang Bang
Bada Bing malls
Tanning stalls
Gotcha by the balls.

Speed up the Turnpike
To embrace a city
That named us Jerseyites
The Bridge & Tunnel crowd.

You gotta pay to get into
claustrophobic tunnels
and massive, steeled bridges
But they send us back for free!

Bada Bing

Hoboken ain't New Jersey
It's Village meets Bowery
With just a Little Italy
Giving it some sauce

In Jersey we go shuffle
Tawking Springsteen and Soprano.
Boys living off trust funds and big hair.
Play in Rock & Roll bands at Pizza joints.

Go-Go bars, fast food
keep the truck stops in business.
Cute girls down the shore
Each outlap-dancing the other.

In Jersey we Bang Bang but good

Don't argue with a Jersey Girl
Don't kiss a Jersey Boy
And don't expect your calls to be returned.

You guys, don't be messing with Jersey.
You'll be passing through
to get to Florida when you're old.
leaving the city for big sunglasses and sun?

Bada Bing.

Resolution

Once, I sliced my right wrist
to make sure I had the same insides
as everyone else.
I never felt the cut.

I wasn't prepared to be ordinary.
Mother said I wouldn't be.
Father didn't say much —
he just used his fists.

Do you feel sorry for me? Don't.
Flesh knows how to heal,
unlike the rest of me.
Working on it made me extraordinary.

While birthing my own daughter
I hollered "Oh fuck!" until the doctors
brought me Darvon. I took it,
but not for pain. Pain keeps me company.

What do you do with a girl?
Tell her there's money in go-go bars
and relief in drugs? That one day
her body may get her a lot of things?

The little scar still rides my right wrist,
a reminder that I'm stronger than any situation.
That I am extraordinary.

You don't have to agree.

How to View a Decade

There is a carnal fluidity
in viewing a decade.

It masquerades as sweet musk
on layers of tissue, dulled

photographs, smooth stone.
Bric-a-brac.

Memory unwraps them.
Memory sometimes chooses its way

like a prospectus — the decade
a mere sketch of itself, drawn clean,

erased of sleep or stillness. Inside
a decade of youth is a smoldering

cinder, a pile of ashed flesh
and heat. Wrapped in soft pink tissue.

Trinkets commemorate, screen
defective parts out. This is how to view a decade:

A carnal weeping out. Escaped heat.
The end of it preserved in pressed

things. Leaves and concert stubs. Four leaf
clovers. Musty hotel receipts.

A Slow Wet Thaw

Raw, nude, vibrating,
Absorbed of pulsing shudder.
Moist between thigh and brain,
infectious purgatory ache—
A pulsing wound that
draws what is close
even closer.

Couldn't I escape you,
pulling my limbs wide?
But you return to your lover
while I imagine your hands
as they were, carnal.
I cover myself in
blankets of them.
This slight thaw, a slow wet—
must now be
enough to remember.

Thoughts of your tongue
flush downwards,
unfold my hips.
You weren't looking.
God, your eyes, your eyes
forcing my fingers down,
tick tick tick ticking. It
drags you home, panting.

A pulling away. One damn pull
saves this descent.
Draw blinds in mind's house.
Draw blinds in mind.

How minds draw blinds till
blindness becomes the
newer wound.

The Passing of Things

"You sit to have waves rush to your open hands and you're surprised as cities grow there..." – Jim Carroll (from "To a Poetess")

Blue light in mirror — a reflection of sorts:
Razor words on melancholy tongue.

Everything has changed, this generation game played out.
Flashbacks of blue, my eyes ribboned,

tied like parcels. My bouquet for you.
My requiem. For you. The fragility of us

leaves me wanting. Why does it surprise
to learn of the passing of things? Oh, those elusive words —

damn it! I wanted to say something worthy.
But all I hold is this light, blue as your eyes,

slowly settling and disappearing, as all things do.
Maybe I wasn't meant to learn the words

only hold each minute, each second.
Our lives crossing like a sacrament,

my words etched with yours by proxy.
And blue. Blue as your eyes.

Your God Forbids

Master fire, instigator thigh.
Whiff of drink
and smoke.
Tight as elastic band,
soul asphyxiated right at
the neck
and you with your
no-holding lack of
control issues.

We're all insecure.
Master gunner:
machine gun tongue.
Exquisite hands
have not touched enough
to resolve to climax, yet
settle at your groin.
And now my neck.
Wring it dry
so no words have
want
ever again.

You knifed the poet's legs apart.
Drained her alphabet,
bled her when all you wanted
was a tongue soft
over yours.
But your God forbids
We live as flesh.
his elastic tightens,
renders you lifeless.

Toddy Idol

Todd, we danced through
the Eighties, you in kilt and Docs:
the shaman of decadent punk.

You made playgrounds of us all
and we happily obliged.
When AIDS came to claim you
we pretended not to notice as you
shrunk into your spiked hair.
We refused the dark circles
and rashes no makeup could hide.
We kept dancing.
It was all we knew how to do.

What you wanted was easy breath,
a continued ride on the swings.
Healing from the latest round of gay-bashing
was easy compared to the beatings AIDS dealt,
that toughest of bullies.

We stopped laughing so hard, and took off the Docs.
I found them in a closet yesterday.
Thought it might be time to toss them out.

I saved them as a way to keep you dancing.

Transition

In the end it comes down to
letting go.

Big, fat chunks of it. Bones with meat
still clinging.
Detached from frame of soul
that nurtured yet still was turned away.

In the end they grow away, separate
which was always the goal
but the blade is never the less sharp
and precise.

In the end it boils down, into soft stew.
Not as tasty, but small bites appreciated.

The feel of life beginning somewhere within
has changed to one starting
very much apart.
Resentment surprises me.

I expected release.
To find myself somewhere amidst
brave new world and confidant.
Instead, I have found neither world fits.
I am cooked.

Mustard Love Song

It wasn't mustard that ruined us.
This September day I walk,
thinking of changing landscapes.
Picnic calm is shelved
until sun warms it once again.
That's the way it is. That's all.
This inability to control the climate of marriage
Permeates this silence,
replacing the words that never
found their home here.

I packed my heart away long ago
in this condiment country.
I didn't want Labor Day —
I wanted a life of seasons. Celebrations.
Silly cards. And, damn it, I wanted flowers!
Big, beautiful bunches bleeding color
into my hands as I wash them.
Instead, this day you gave me shade.
It wasn't mustard — or lack of.
It wasn't that you stopped mowing
and forgot home was bigger than a pit stop.

Our house grew larger, engulfed me, drained me
Until I was empty. So empty my palms
dragged full out of steam into autumn,
dirtier than the stain I got on your shirt
when a loose lid let loose.
Because I wanted flowers.
And not because I asked for them.

Doing the Math

Here's what I know:
A circle leads back to itself
so as never to join completely
with another.
Dead weight is a leaden sphere
that wishes to be a circle.
I do not wish to run into myself,
indefinitely, indefinitely, indefinitely...

Center point radius — what is the circumference?
How many, what?
Fraction is to arc, OR...
one half, what is one half?
Configure!
Concentric circles, separate or conjoined?
Slice!
Left side relates how? To right?
I wish not to be right.

Nor a circle. Nor a circle. Nor a circle. Nor a circle.

I wish to smash theory!
Pull pages so problem
is neither resolved nor steadied
but thought about.

Here's what I saw:
x is to y as y is to z and if we were algebra
I might first have to know you better to understand
z needs y to make sense of x.

A genius could figure out the distance between us.

But only a genius.

Draw Me a Cover

Rene, you are in Brooklyn counting losses.
Surrounded by canvas and sketches.
Living in remnants from your SoHo loft,
memories stuffed into boxes and folders.

I promised to pick you up,
bring you back to Spring Street
where we dined weekly at Food
and drew our futures on napkins.

I want to twist your hair back into devil horns
but it has faded into wisps that you cover.
You tell me inspiration has eluded you.
Ideas dry as old paint on a palette.

I am angry that what we said we were going to do
we are doing and now your sadness
has turned your Venezualen skin pale.
Draw me a cover, my friend. A fine cover.

It will sit on top of my small poems
and keep you part of our pact.
Draw me a lady who is part of this world
yet separate. But keep on drawing.

Your name still sweeps across Wooster Street
in rainbow colors. The paint has faded,
the letters have bent with so many winters.
But that is what years do to people and things.

Draw me a cover Rene,
draw me a woman with fire in her eyes.

About the Author

International wordrocker and spoken word artist Cyndi Dawson curates the Poets and Angels music and poetry series. She has worked as an actress in TV and film and as a performance artist, famous for her collaboration with Venezuelan, SoHo-based, artist Rene in the 1980s. Cyndi has stood in for Madonna, appeared on *Law and Order*, Advil commercials and numerous films and TV series.

She has performed all over NY/NJ at such venues as the Bowery Poetry Club, The Cornelia Street Café, Tribal Spears Gallery in Harlem, and St. Marks in NYC and the Grassroots Arts Facility in Jersey City as well as in Europe. She recently read at the Poetry Cafe in London, Maggie's Bar in Stoke-Newington , the King Henry VI in Eton and at Feile in Dublin, Ireland. Her spoken word has been featured in the *Going Down Swinging* CD and has been heard on radio stations around the world. She has been featured in *The Pulse Entertainment Magazine*, *The Star Ledger*, *The Home News Tribune* and *The Reporter*.

Cyndi's poetry has been published in many, many anthologies and publications including *Gutter Eloquence Magazine*, *Heroin Love Songs*, *Lines Written with a Razor*, *Spine Writer*, *Deep Tissue Magazine*, *Off Beat Pulp*, *Breadcrumb Scabs*, *The Plebian Rag*, *63 Channels*, *The Skyline 2009 Review*, *The Aquarian*, *Images of the Mystic Truth*, *Gloom Cupboard*, *Light Trauma*, *Journey of the Poet/Prophet*, *Poetz.com* and the *Livingston Medium*. Her two previous books of poetry are *Dream Sequences* and *Inside of Outside*.

Visit her online at www.myspace.com/insideofoutside.

www.ingramcontent.com/pod-product-compliance
Lightning Source LLC
Chambersburg PA
CBHW061759040426
42447CB00011B/2376